THE LAME M
WHO WALKED AGAIN

ATTHEW 9:2-8 FOR CHILDREN

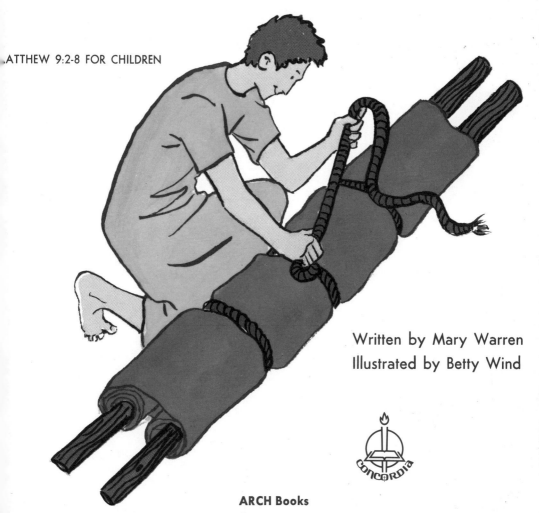

Written by Mary Warren
Illustrated by Betty Wind

ARCH Books

© 1966 CONCORDIA PUBLISHING HOUSE, ST. LOUIS, MISSOURI
CONCORDIA PUBLISHING HOUSE LTD., LONDON, E. C. 1
MANUFACTURED IN THE UNITED STATES OF AMERICA
ALL RIGHTS RESERVED
ISBN 0-570-06020-6

When Jesus taught in Galilee,
a lot of people came
because they heard that He could heal
the deaf, the blind, the lame,

the folks who could not talk at all,
and some on stretcher beds,
and those with fits and stomachaches,
and others with hurt heads.

Some mothers carried babies small
too sick to make a cry.
And Jesus healed the lepers too,
and any passing by
who had a fever, crippled arm,
or any kind of pain.
And people who were feeling sad
He soon made laugh again!

There was one man who could not move.
He wept,
he wanted so
to go to Jesus to be healed.
He watched the others go.

His wife went out to ask his friends
if they might find a way.
"Why sure!" they cried, "We'll carry him.
Come! Let us go today!"

They packed a lunch, then grabbed his bed,
and started down the road.
"Take heart," one laughed,
"We'll soon be there.
This isn't such a load!"

"I think I know the house," one called,
"It isn't hard to tell.
I see a mob of people there . . .
and some already well!"

Sure enough—one man had thrown
his crutch away in glee;
and another shouted out:
"My eyes are healed! I see!"

But when the friends got to the house
they could not reach the door.
So many people crowded in
there was no room for more.

"Don't give up, we'll find a way;
we won't go home," they said.
So, as they walked around the house,
the man watched from his bed.

At last one had a clever thought.
"Oho! the roof!" he cried.

"Now hang on tight and up we'll go!
O! What a bumpy ride!"
To hoist the sick man to the roof
they tugged with all their might.
A few who stood there watching smiled
at this unusual sight.

"These tiles are loose; let's take them off and lower him right down!"

The startled people in the house
jumped back: "Who is this clown?"

But Jesus watched how tenderly
the friends set down the bed.
He saw the sad and worried eyes
the sick man had, and said,
with kindness in His voice: "My son,
your sins I take away."
Some people thought: "This cannot be!
Is this for man to say?

"It's only God who can forgive.
That right is only His!
This man is rather arrogant.
Who does He think He is?"

But Jesus said:
"I can forgive!
It's not a bunch of lies.
I'll show you what I mean:
Young man,
fold up your stretcher!
Rise!"

The sick man up
and shouted: "Thanks!"
He danced around in joy.
He hadn't felt so full of life
since he had been a boy!

He tied his stretcher in a roll;
the people watched, amazed.
They raised their hands toward heaven high
and cried out: "God be praised!

"What Jesus says is true! Just look!
This man whom He forgives is well!
Let's hurry back to all our friends . . .
We have good news to tell!"

DEAR PARENTS:

Jesus was concerned about the whole man — not just about his soul or just about his physical well-being. But because the different parts of man hang together, Jesus heals both body and soul.

Our story shows Jesus' love and understanding of each man and his troubles. The Gospel doesn't claim that our lame man was sick because he had committed some sin (otherwise we would all have to be sick all of our lives). But Jesus sensed the burden of guilt the lame man was secretly carrying. That is why Jesus forgave the man before healing him.

The main point of the Gospel here is that Jesus has the authority to forgive on God's behalf. We don't just *hope* that God will forgive. We receive the *certainty* of our forgiveness through the Savior He has sent and those who act in His name. (John 20:21-23)

Can you help your child think of Jesus as someone who can and does forgive us when we have been bad, so that the past is past and we can move about with the carefree heart and confidence which belongs to God's children? And will you help him sense the reality of God's forgiveness by accepting God's forgiveness yourself for your own failures and those of others, especially in your own family?

THE EDITOR